Your Favorite Hymns *for* Guitar *Book One*

Arranged by ERNIE ALLEE

Compiled by R. W. Stringfield
Edited by Floyd W. Hawkins

CONTENTS

In this book only one stanza of the words appears with each hymn
Complete texts may be obtained in the book *50 Hymns America Loves Best,*
available from your music supplier or the publishers.

Lillenas Publishing Co.

KANSAS CITY, MO. 64141

GUITAR CHORDS

Fingering Diagrams of Chords Used in This Book

THE MAJOR CHORDS

○=Open string

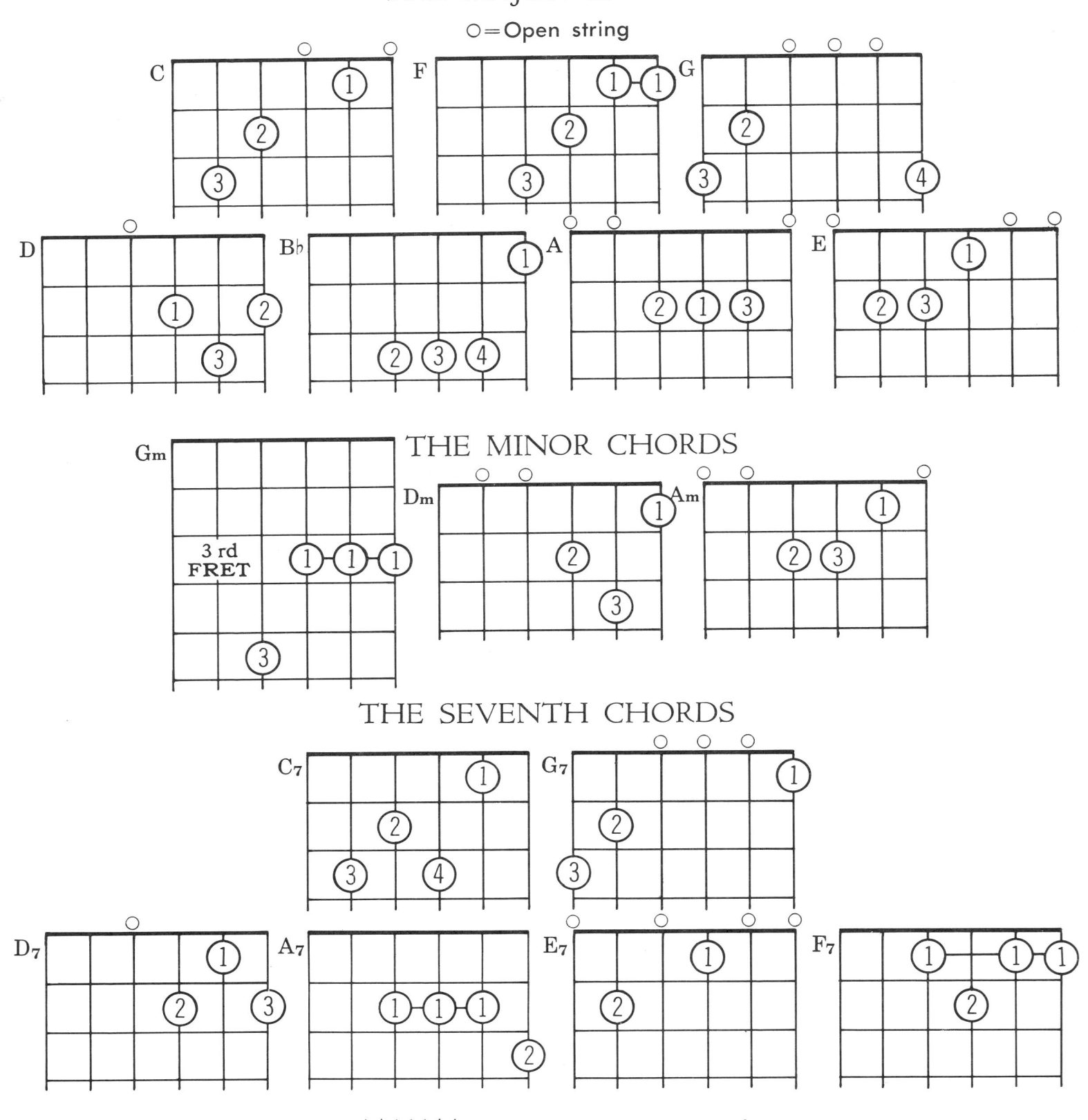

THE MINOR CHORDS

THE SEVENTH CHORDS

//////// = Stroke marks for the pick

The Beautiful Garden of Prayer

ELEANOR ALLEN SCHROLL   J. H. FILLMORE

Whispering Hope

A. H.

Arr. from **ALICE HAWTHORNE**

Soft as the voice of an an - gel, Breath - ing a les - son un - heard,_____ Hope with a gen - tle per - sua - sion Whis - pers her com - fort - ing word:_____ "Wait till the dark - ness is o - ver; Wait till the tem - pest is done;_____ Hope for the sun - shine to - mor - row, Af - ter the show - er is gone."_____

I Need Thee Every Hour

ANNIE S. HAWKS

ROBERT LOWRY

Jesus, Lover of My Soul

CHARLES WESLEY

SIMEON B. MARSH

Je-sus, Lov-er of my soul, Let me to Thy bos-om fly,

While the near-er wa-ters roll, While the tem-pest still is high!

Hide me, O my Sav-iour, hide, Till the storm of life is past.

Safe in-to the ha-ven guide. Oh, re-ceive my soul at last!

Sweet By and By

S. F. BENNETT

J. P. WEBSTER

There's a land that is fair-er than day, And by faith we can see it a-

far: For the Fa-ther waits o-ver the way, To pre-pare us a dwell-ing place there.

REFRAIN

In the sweet by and by, We shall meet on that beau-ti-ful

shore. In the sweet by and by, We shall meet on that beau-ti-ful shore.

What a Friend

JOSEPH SCRIVEN

CHARLES C. CONVERSE

What a Friend we have in Je-sus, All our sins and griefs to bear!

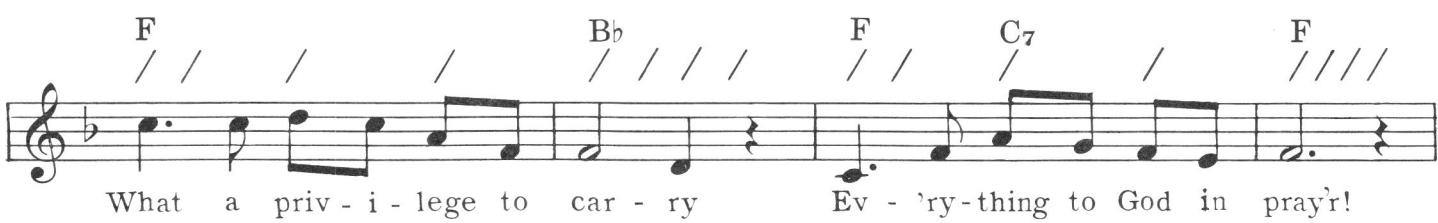

What a priv-i-lege to car-ry Ev-'ry-thing to God in pray'r!

Oh, what peace we of-ten for-feit, Oh, what need-less pain we bear,

All be-cause we do not car-ry Ev-'ry-thing to God in pray'r!

My Faith Looks Up to Thee

RAY PALMER

LOWELL MASON

My faith looks up to Thee, Thou Lamb of Cal - va - ry, Sav - iour di - vine! Now hear me while I pray, Take all my guilt a - way. Oh, let me from this day Be whol - ly Thine!

Jesus, Saviour, Pilot Me

EDWARD HOPPER

JOHN E. GOULD

Je - sus, Sav - iour, pi - lot me O - ver life's tem - pes - tuous sea. Un - known waves be - fore me roll, Hid - ing rocks and treach - 'rous shoal. Chart and com - pass came from Thee; Je - sus, Sav - iour, pi - lot me.

Abide with Me

HENRY F. LYTE

WILLIAM H. MONK

Amazing Grace

JOHN NEWTON

Early American Melody

Onward, Christian Soldiers

SABINE BARING-GOULD

ARTHUR S. SULLIVAN

Rock of Ages

AUGUSTUS M. TOPLADY

THOMAS HASTINGS

Nearer, My God, to Thee

SARAH F. ADAMS

LOWELL MASON

Lead, Kindly Light

JOHN H. NEWMAN   JOHN B. DYKES

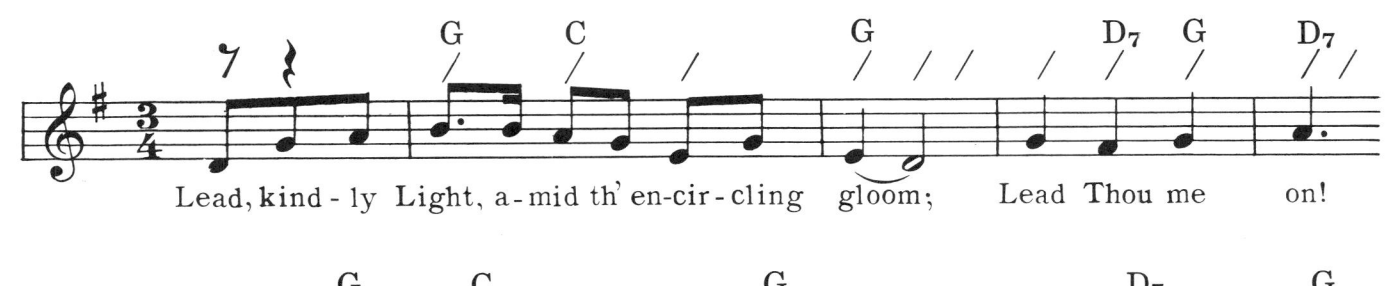

Lead, kind-ly Light, a-mid th' en-cir-cling gloom; Lead Thou me on!

The night is dark, and I am far from home; Lead Thou me on!

Keep Thou my feet; I do not ask to see

The dis-tant scene; one step e-nough for me.

God Will Take Care of You

C. D. MARTIN   W. S. MARTIN

Be not dis-mayed what-e'er be-tide; God will take care of you.

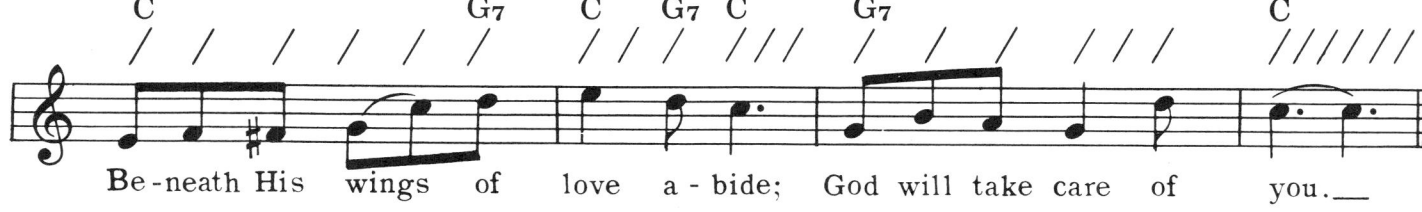

Be-neath His wings of love a-bide; God will take care of you.

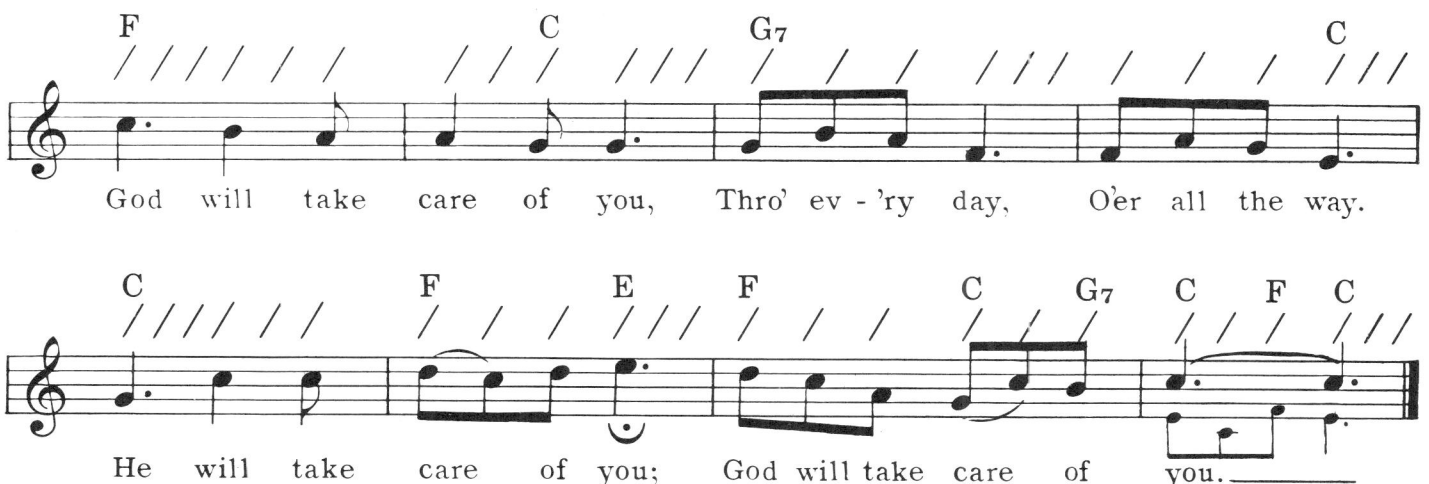

REFRAIN

F C G7 C
God will take care of you, Thro' ev - 'ry day, O'er all the way.
C F E F C G7 C F C
He will take care of you; God will take care of you.

Holy, Holy, Holy

REGINALD HEBER

JOHN B. DYKES

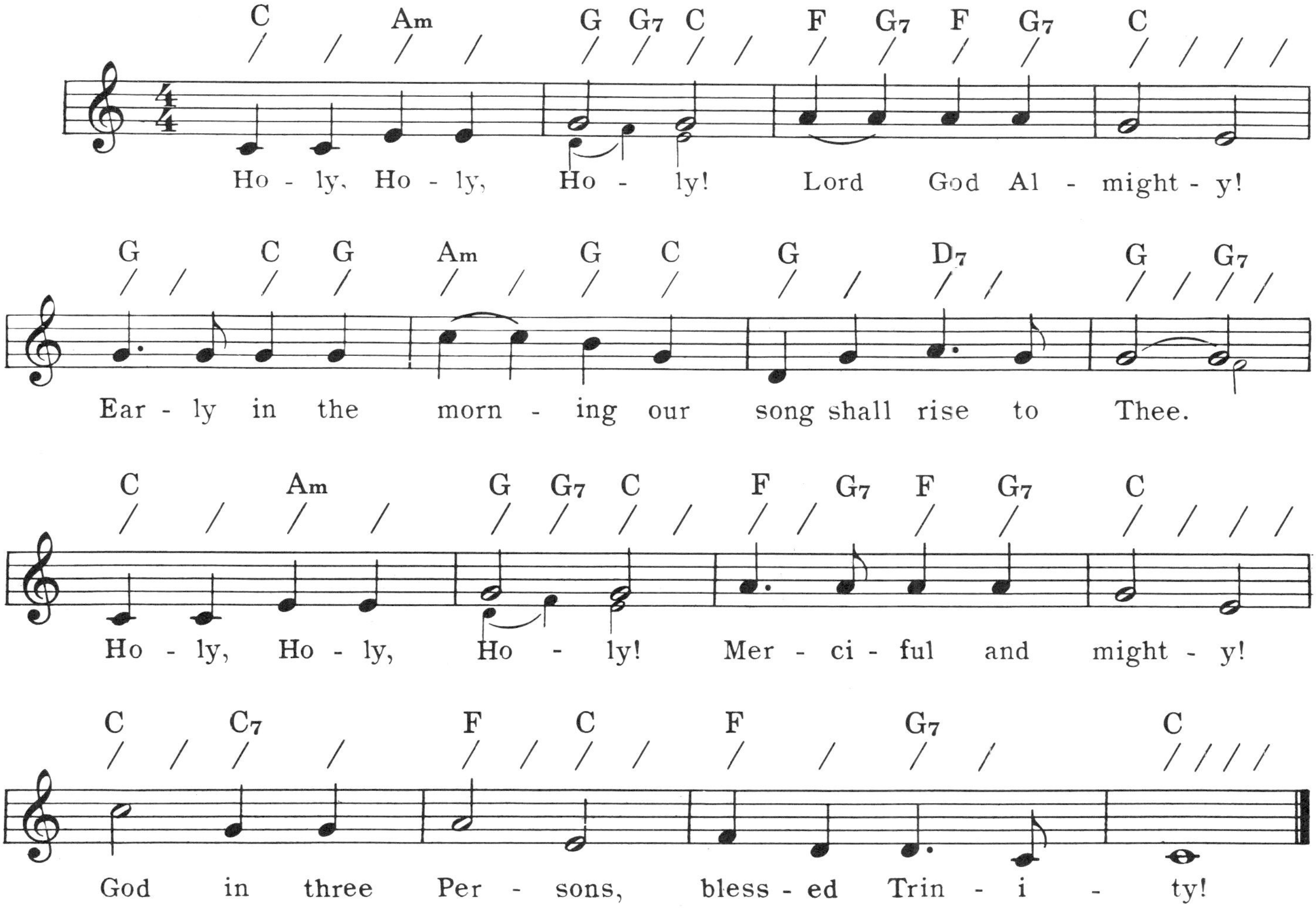

C Am G G7 C F G7 F G7 C
Ho - ly, Ho - ly, Ho - ly! Lord God Al - might - y!
G C G Am G C G D7 G G7
Ear - ly in the morn - ing our song shall rise to Thee.
C Am G G7 C F G7 F G7 C
Ho - ly, Ho - ly, Ho - ly! Mer - ci - ful and might - y!
C C7 F C F G7 C
God in three Per - sons, bless - ed Trin - i - ty!

Blessed Assurance

FANNY J. CROSBY

Mrs. JOS. F. KNAPP

The Love of God

F. M. L.

F. M. LEHMAN

I Love to Tell the Story

KATHERINE HANKEY

WILLIAM G. FISCHER

I love to tell the sto - ry Of un - seen things a -
bove, Of Je - sus and His glo - ry, Of Je - sus and His
love. I love to tell the sto - ry Be - cause I know 'tis
true. It sat - is - fies my long - ings As noth - ing else can do.

REFRAIN

I love to tell the sto - ry! 'Twill be my theme in glo - ry
To tell the old, old sto - ry Of Je - sus and His love.

Take Time to Be Holy

W. D. LONGSTAFF

GEO. C. STEBBINS

Take time to be ho - ly; Speak oft with thy Lord.____

A - bide in Him al - ways, And feed on His Word.____

Make friends of God's chil - dren: Help those who are weak,____

For - get - ting in noth - ing His bless - ing to seek.____

Just as I Am

CHARLOTTE ELLIOTT

WILLIAM B. BRADBURY

Just as I am____ with - out____ one plea But

that____ Thy blood was shed for me And that Thou bidd'st____ me

come to Thee,____ O Lamb of God____ I come! I come!____

O Mighty God
"O Store Gud"

Swedish Folk Melody

Publisher's Note—
    This melody, with the Swedish poem "O Store Gud," by Carl Gustaf Boberg, was published as a hymn late in the nineteenth century. The version now popular in America and Great Britain is a translation by Stuart K. Hine, "How Great Thou Art!" Restrictions placed on the United States copyright of this translation prevented its use in this book.

Sweet Hour of Prayer

W. W. WALFORD

Wm. G. BRADBURY

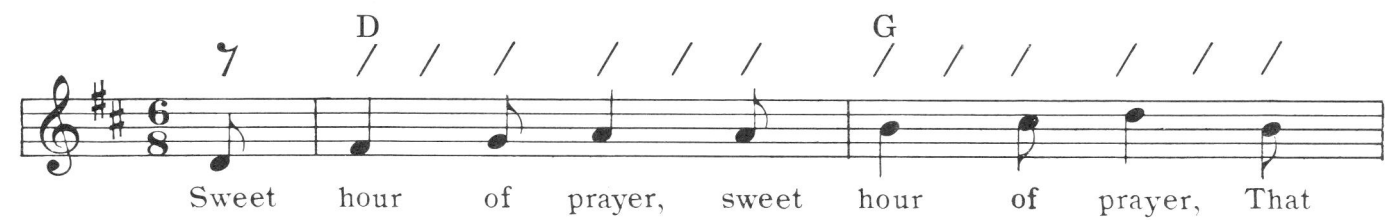

Sweet hour of prayer, sweet hour of prayer, That

calls me from a world of care And bids me at my

Fa - ther's throne Make all my wants and wish - es known! In

sea - sons of dis - tress and grief My soul has of - ten

found re - lief, And oft es - caped the temp - ter's snare

By thy re - turn, sweet hour of prayer.

Just a Closer Walk with Thee

Spiritual

This Is My Father's World

MALTBIE D. BABCOCK

FRANKLIN L. SHEPPARD

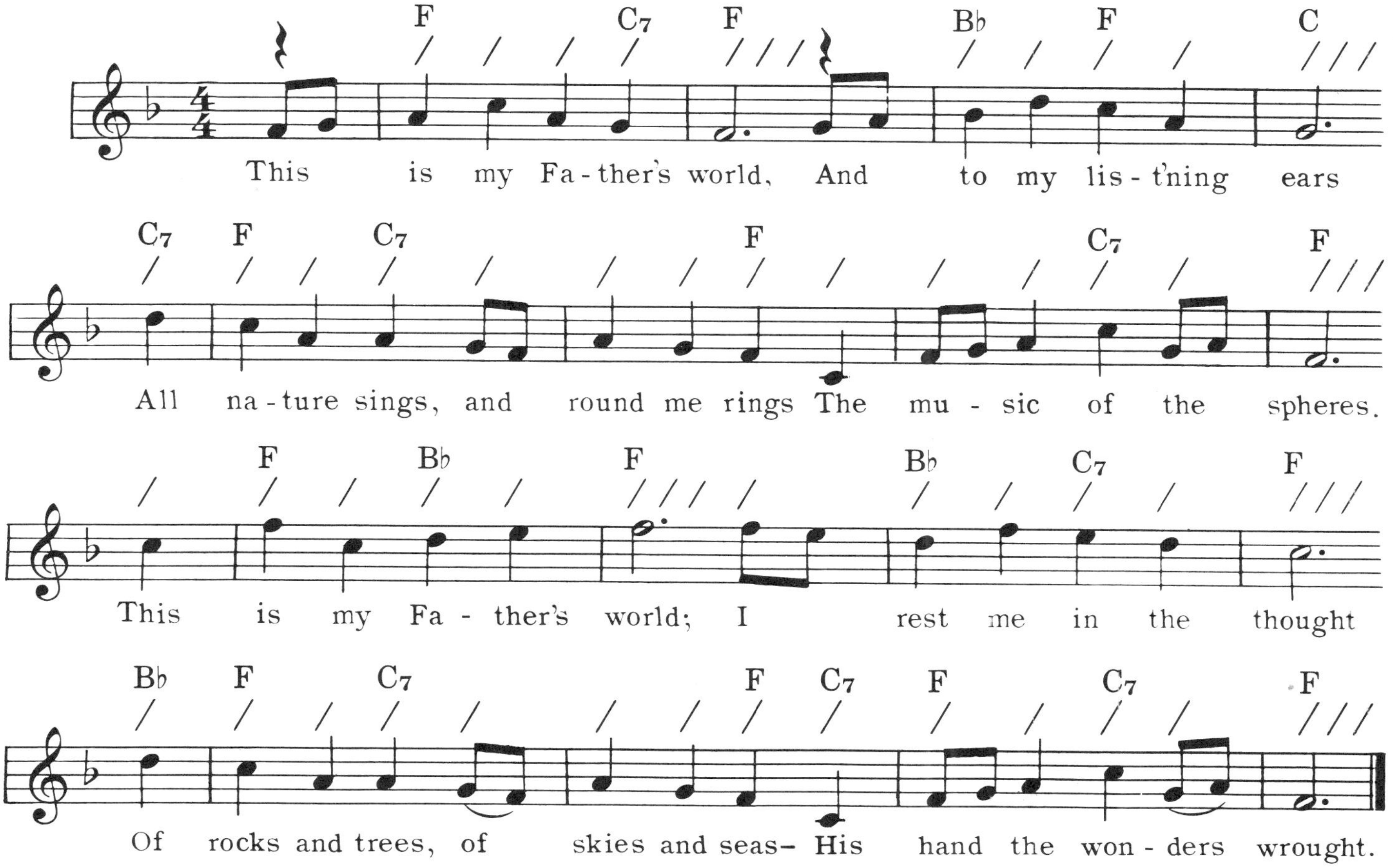
F C7 F Bb F C
This is my Fa-ther's world, And to my lis-t'ning ears
C7 F C7 F C7 F
All na-ture sings, and round me rings The mu-sic of the spheres.
F Bb F Bb C7 F
This is my Fa-ther's world; I rest me in the thought
Bb F C7 F C7 F C7 F
Of rocks and trees, of skies and seas– His hand the won-ders wrought.

When I Survey the Wondrous Cross

ISAAC WATTS

LOWELL MASON

F C F Gm D7 Gm F C F
When I sur-vey the___ won-drous Cross, On which the
Bb F C7 F C7 F C F C F Gm D7
Prince of___ Glo-ry___ died, My rich-est gain I___
Gm F C F Dm C C7 Dm Gm C7 F
count but___ loss, And pour con-tempt on all my___ pride.

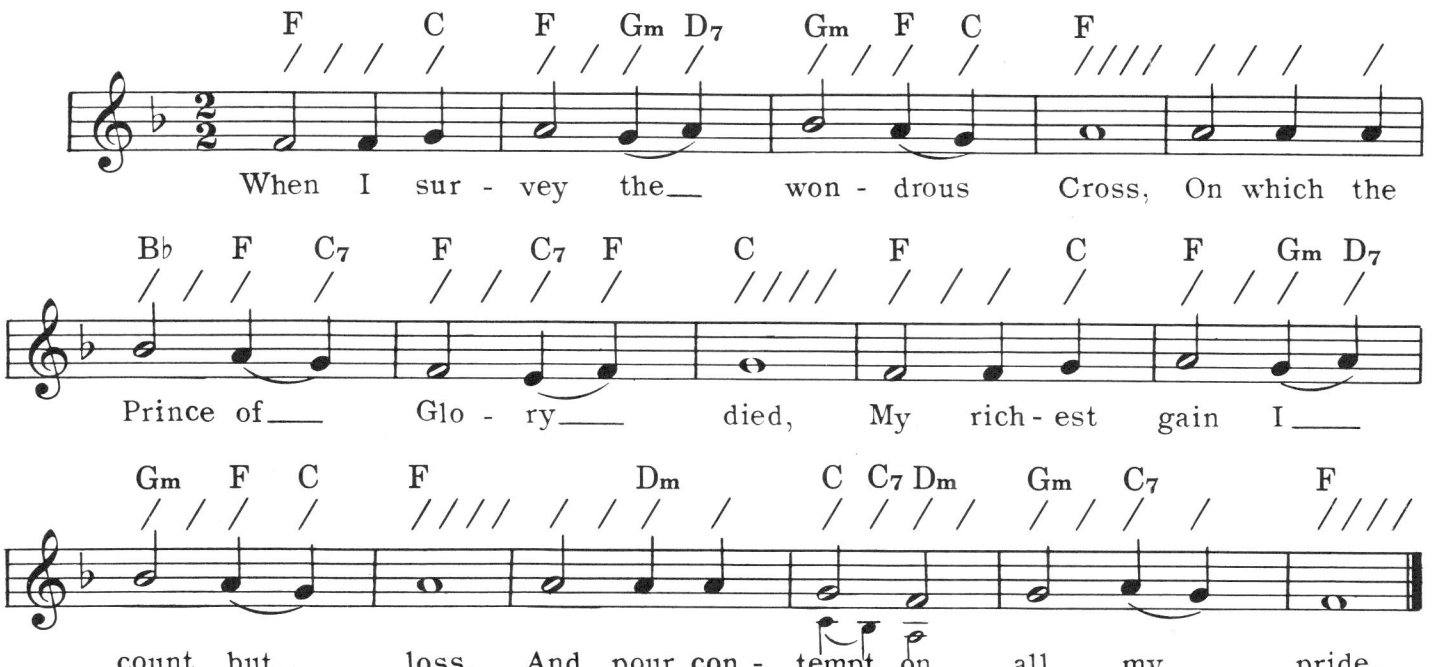

"Are Ye Able?" Said the Master

EARL MARLATT

HARRY S. MASON

Near the Cross

FANNY J. CROSBY

WILLIAM H. DOANE

Je - sus, keep me near the Cross. There a pre - cious foun - tain,

Free to all, a heal - ing stream, Flows from Cal - v'ry's moun - tain.

REFRAIN

In the Cross, in the Cross, Be my glo - ry ev - er,

Till my rap - tured soul shall find Rest be - yond the riv - er.

Blest Be the Tie

JOHN FAWCETT

H. G. NAGELI

Blest be ___ the tie ___ that binds Our hearts in

Chris - tian love; The fel - low - ship ___ of

kin - dred minds Is like ___ to that ___ a - bove.

Be Still, My Soul

KATHARINA von SCHLEGEL
Tr. by Jane L. Borthwick

JEAN SIBELIUS

Be still, my soul; the Lord is on thy side.

Bear pa - tient - ly the cross of grief or pain;

Leave to thy God to or - der and pro - vide;

In ev - 'ry change He faith - ful will re - main.

Be still, my soul; thy best, thy heav'n - ly Friend

Thro' thorn - y ways leads to a joy - ful end.

Near to the Heart of God

C. B. McAFEE

There is a place of qui - et rest, Near to the heart of

God: A place where sin can - not mo-lest, Near to the heart of God.

REFRAIN

O Je - sus, blest Re - deem - er, Sent from the heart of God,

Hold us, who wait be - fore Thee, Near to the heart of God.

Fairest Lord Jesus

From the German, 17th Century

From "Schlesische Volkslieder"

Fair - est Lord Je - sus! Rul - er of all na - ture!

O Thou of God and man the Son! Thee will I cher - ish,

Thee will I hon - or, Thou, my soul's glo - ry, joy, and crown!

Faith of Our Fathers

FREDERICK W. FABER

HENRI F. HEMY
and J. G. WALTON

Faith of our fa - thers, liv - ing still

In spite of dun - geon, fire, ___ and sword!

Oh, how our hearts ___ beat high ___ with joy

When - e'er we hear that glo - rious word!

Faith of our fa - thers! ho - ly faith!

We will be true to thee till death!

While Shepherds Watched

NAHUM TATE

From GEORGE F. HANDEL

While shep-herds watched their flocks by night, All seat-ed on the ground, The an-gel of the Lord came down. And glo-ry shone a-round, And glo-ry shone a-round.

Angels, from the Realms of Glory

JAMES MONTGOMERY

HENRY SMART

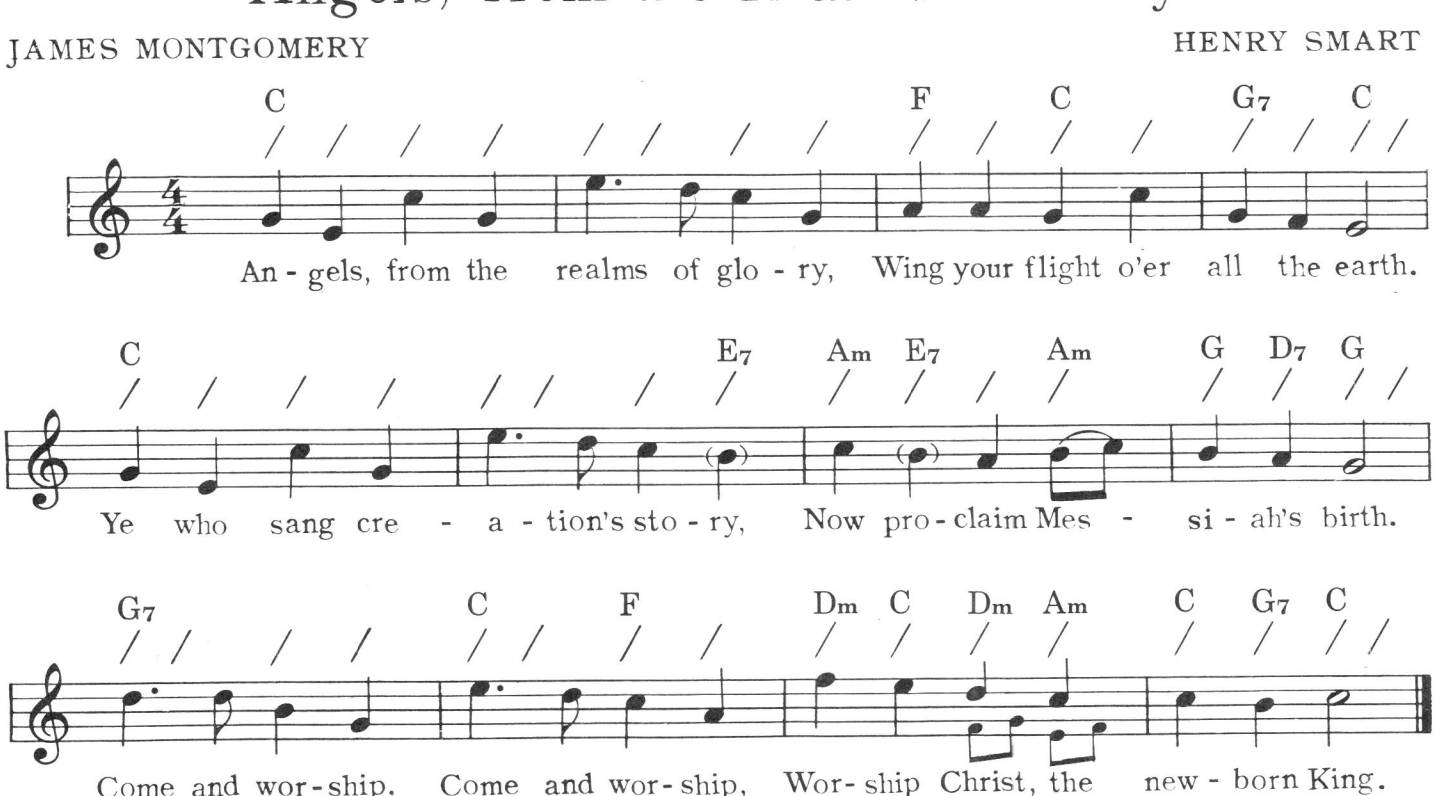

An-gels, from the realms of glo-ry, Wing your flight o'er all the earth. Ye who sang cre-a-tion's sto-ry, Now pro-claim Mes-si-ah's birth. Come and wor-ship. Come and wor-ship, Wor-ship Christ, the new-born King.

Silent Night

JOSEPH MOHR

FRANZ GRUBER

C / / / /// / / G7 / /
Si - lent night! Ho - ly night! All is

G7 / / C / / C7 / / F / / /
calm, all is bright Round yon vir - gin

C / / / /// F / /
moth - er and Child! Ho - ly In - fant, so

C / / /// G7 / / / C ///
ten - der and mild, Sleep in heav - en - ly peace.

C /// / G7 / / C /// ///
Sleep___ in heav - en - ly peace.___

O Little Town of Bethlehem

PHILLIPS BROOKS

LEWIS H. REDNER

F / / / Bb / / F C7 / / F ////
O lit - tle town of Beth - le - hem, How still we see thee lie! A -

F / D7 / Gm / / / F / C7 / F ////
bove thy deep and dream - less sleep The si - lent stars go by. Yet

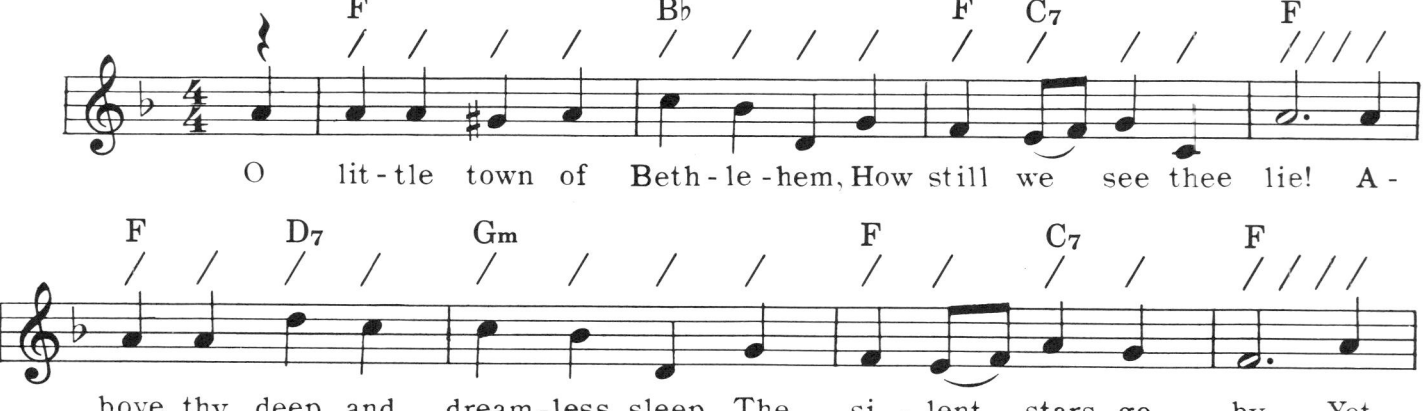

in thy dark streets shin - eth The ev - er - last - ing Light; The

hopes and fears of all the years Are met in thee to - night.

Oh, Come, All Ye Faithful

Tr. by Frederick Oakeley

Wade's "Cantus Diversi"

Oh, come, all ye faith - ful, joy - ful and tri - um - phant! Oh,

come ye, oh, come ye to Beth - le - hem.

Come and be - hold Him, born the King of an - gels.

REFRAIN

Oh, come, let us a - dore Him! Oh, come, let us a - dore Him! Oh,

come, let us a - dore Him,___ Christ,___ the Lord!

Joy to the World

ISAAC WATTS

From GEORGE F. HANDEL

Joy to the world, the Lord is come! Let earth re-
ceive her King; Let ev - 'ry heart___ pre - pare__ Him___
room,___ And heav'n and na - ture sing, And heav'n and na - ture
sing, And heav'n, and heav'n___ and na - ture sing.

Hark! The Herald Angels Sing

CHARLES WESLEY

FELIX MENDELSSOHN

Hark! The her - ald an - gels sing, "Glo - ry to the new-born King!
Peace on earth, and mer - cy mild; God and sin - ners rec - on - ciled."
Joy - ful, all ye na - tions, rise; Join the tri - umph of the skies;

The First Noel

Old English Carol

Traditional Melody

With th'an-gel-ic hosts pro-claim, "Christ is born in Beth-le-hem."

Hark! The her-ald an-gels sing, "Glo-ry to the new-born King."

The first No-el the an-gels did say Was to cer-tain poor shep-herds in fields as they lay; In fields where they lay keep-ing their sheep, On a cold win-ter's night that

REFRAIN

was so deep. No-el, No-el, No-el, No-el, Born is the King of Is-ra-el.

It Came upon the Midnight Clear

EDMUND H. SEARS

RICHARD S. WILLIS

It came up - on____ the mid - night clear, That
glo - rious song __ of old, ____ From an - gels bend - ing
near the earth To touch their harps __ of gold: ____
"Peace on the earth, ____ good will to men, From
heav'n's all - gra - cious King." ____ The world in sol - emn
still - ness lay To hear the an - gels sing. ____